The Love of Grace

Susan Leffler

ISBN: 0990624404

ISBN 13: 9780990624400

Library of Congress Control Number: 2014913357

CreateSpace Independent Publishing Platform

North Charleston, South Carolina

I dedicate this little book to all of God's children,
young and old. May His love and joy be planted deep
into your hearts and produce abundant fruit of the same.

Acknowledgements

I want to thank my husband Chris for being a constant source of love and encouragement all along this journey. I also want to thank Elisabeth Cooper for encouraging me to step out of the box in my artwork and to write this book. But most of all, I thank Father God for His love, His grace, His Son and for giving me Gracie. Thank you Papa.

Hi, my name is Grace, but everyone calls me Gracie. This is my puppy Oscar. Everyone calls him cute!

I want to tell you about God's love and joy.

In order to know how much someone loves you, you have to get to know them. It's the same way with God the Father.

God and I have a special relationship. Sometimes I call Him Papa and sometimes He calls me Gracie.

And we have known and believed the love God has for us.
God is love, and he who abides in love abides in God and God in him.

1John 4:16

When I spend quiet time with God, I say "I love you Papa", and He says, "I love you too Gracie". Then I feel God's love surrounding me like a warm soft blanket.

But the water that I shall give him will become in him
a fountain of water springing up into everlasting life.

John 4:14

God's love is like a fountain.

It's always on, it never runs out, it fills us with the confidence we need that we can do anything because He is always there with us to help us.

And knowing the love God has for us just fills us up till it spills over onto others.

God's love for us is deeper than the ocean…

...is wider than the Grand Canyon...

...is higher than the stars...

10

...and it never, never ends!

Two thousand years ago God showed us how much
He loves us by sending His Son Jesus.

For God so loved the world that He gave His only begotten Son,
that whoever believes in Him should not perish but have everlasting life.
John 3:16

Jesus showed us how to love and what love is and how great we
can be and the great things we can do when we know God's love.

Love suffers long and is kind; love does not envy; love does not parade itself, is not puffed up;
does not behave rudely, does not seek its own, is not provoked, thinks no evil; does not rejoice
in iniquity, but rejoices in truth; bears all things, endures all things. Love never fails...
1Cor 13:4-8

When we lend a helping hand to someone, when we give to
someone who doesn't have, when we befriend someone, when we
give encouraging words, we are extending God's love to others.

If we love one another, God abides in us and His love has been perfected in us.
1John 4:12

God treasures our hearts. We are all precious to Him.

We hold God near to us because He is our treasure.

For where your treasure is, there your heart will be also.
Luke 12:34

God loves us so much that we are called His children. Young, old, black, white, tall, short, big, small and everyone in between...it doesn't matter to God.

He loves us all!

I think He even has pictures of us on His mantel!

Then Peter opened his mouth and said: "In truth I perceive that God shows no partiality."
Acts 10:34

God's love is unconditional.

It's sort of like my puppy Oscar. Oscar loves me no matter what.

God loves me no matter what. Nothing
will separate me from the love of God.

Nothing!

We love Him because He first loved us.
1John 4:19

Whenever I feel afraid, I think about how much God loves me....

There is no fear in love; but perfect love casts out fear...
1John 4:18

Because His perfect love chases away all fear forever.

When you lie down, you will not be afraid; yes you will lie down and your sleep will be sweet.
Prov 3:24

God has blessed us all. That's just what He likes to do.
It makes Him happy, it gives Him joy and it
makes us happy and joyful.

Like when I give Oscar a treat, it makes me
happy and I laugh because he's so full of joy!

Blessed be the God and Father of our Lord Jesus Christ, who has blessed us with every
spiritual blessing in heavenly places in Christ...

Eph 1:3

These things I have spoken to you, that My joy
may remain in you, and that your joy may be full.

John 15:11

If I'm ever sad and confused, I just start to think about how much God loves me and how happy He is with me. His love and joy gives me strength to do the right things and make good choices in my life because I know He is always with me and will never leave me.

The love and joy God has given to me, is meant to give to others. Jesus says, "Freely you have received, freely give".

Jesus taught us that love is the root of all things. That when we know the Fathers love, we will know how to love others and then they will know love and give love to others and that love keeps giving and giving.

It's like a fruit tree that keeps producing fruit all year long.

Love is the fruit that never ends!

...That He would grant you, according to the riches of His glory, to be strengthened with might through His Spirit in the inner man, that Christ may dwell in your hearts through faith; that you being rooted and grounded in love...

Eph 3:16, 17

I have so much love and joy in my heart, that when
I sing to the Lord, I just have to shout it out!

My mom and dad say to me, "All of heaven can hear you
Gracie", but I can hear God say, "You keep singing Gracie.
You put joy in My heart and all of heaven is singing with you."

Shout joyfully to the Lord, all the earth;
break forth in song, rejoice, and sing praises.
Psalm 98:4

Some people tell me, "Gracie, you have the love
and joy of the Lord all over you."

I say, "How can you tell?"

They say, "It's your smile Gracie, your smile says it all!"

God asked me once, "Gracie do you always smile that big?"

I answered, "Only when I'm thinking of you Papa."

You will keep him in perfect peace, whose mind is stayed on You...
Isa 26:3

Accepting Jesus

To know love is to know Jesus. And to know Jesus is to know God the Father, because God is love. If you want to know Jesus and the Father's love, ask Him into your life. He will show you and tell you all about His love for you, just like He did with me. Just say;

"Jesus, I believe in my heart you are the Son of God and that you are my Lord and Savior. I ask you into my life and I receive my salvation now. Thank you Jesus for saving me."

Receive the Holy Spirit

If you just said that prayer and accepted Jesus into your life, or if Jesus is already part of your life, then your loving heavenly Father wants to give you His Holy Spirit.

The Holy Spirit will live in you and will guide you and teach you in the way of the Father. All you have to do is ask, believe and receive.

Just say;

"Father, I ask for your power and your guidance to live this new life you have for me. Please fill me with your Holy Spirit. I receive Him right now. Thank you for baptizing me with your Holy Spirit."

www.ingramcontent.com/pod-product-compliance
Lightning Source LLC
Chambersburg PA
CBHW042121040426
42449CB00003B/131